Second Sun

Second Sun

new and selected poems by
Bill Tremblay

L'Epervier Press

ACKNOWLEDGMENTS

Poems in *Second Sun* were selected from:

Crying in the Cheap Seats, University of Massachusetts Press (Amherst, MA), 1971

The Anarchist Heart, New Rivers Press (New York, NY), 1977

Home Front, Lynx House Press (Amherst, MA), 1978

New Poems (or versions) have appeared in:

The Massachusetts Review, The Minnesota Review, Aloe, Blue Light Review, Prism International, Cincinnatti Poetry Review, Aspen Anthology, The Greenfield Review, Bluefish.

Library of Congress Cataloging in Publication Data:

Tremblay, Bill.
  Second Sun.

  I. Title.
PS3570.R38S4   1985   811'.54   84-26102
ISBN 0-934332-42-8

L'Epervier Press books are distributed by Small Press Distribution, 1784 Shattuck Avenue, Berkeley, California 94709

Cover Photograph, "The Stark Tree," by Wynn Bullock. Used, with thanks, from the collection of Professor and Mrs. Joseph Monsen, Seattle, Washington.

Author's Photograph by Ken Williams, Fort Collins, Colorado.

Book design by Bridget Culligan, Seattle, Washington.

Typeset by Christopher Howell, Vashon, Washington.

Printed by McNaughton & Gunn, Ann Arbor, Michigan.

L'EPERVIER PRESS

CONTENTS

New Poems

ROCK FROM THE FOOTHILLS

In my hands, the rock weighs
many generations, each grain a silicon person.
Inside its crack are the rooms
where we sweated orange from dye-vats,
hoisting huge rolls of parachute nylon.
Bright cones sway down sand-colored skies
to my aunt, viewing my mother's body in the coffin.
"She still looks like a spoiled brat," she says.

My grandfather, dead at 33,
from no child labor laws & tuberculosis & booze
trying to save his imagination singing vaudeville
made my mother his little queen, Irene,
& my Iroquois great-grandmother, "Le Sauvage,"
watched him cough his life out
& smoked her corncob & gave the evil eye
to the french-canadian idea that safe is good.

This rock sounds different
when hit by different memories.
My uncle's small fist makes a cancer sound;
a factory-whistle saying there's no other life
but in the mills
makes the sound of my aunt's children,
stillborn, knocking to get out.

1957

Miss Thecla Fitzgerald stopped time,
made us feel clay & henna & hearth fires dye
the reddleman's leggings
as he sighed for home on a dusty lane.

We knew the fierce dream of city folk
to count pulse in plowed ground
could be carried
on thin black threads
from worlds long buried
to windy Thursday afternoons
in the age of machines.

We knew it was Holy Week,
that the lamb would bleed,
that his Caesar was our Caesar,
that Miss Fitzgerald's voice was the wind
across the moors, speaking from everything
not rendered unto Caesar.

We knew
as we jammed
musical automobiles
that the road & the music were rivers
carrying the dynamo hum of something so big
only telling its story
could keep us from drowning
in the still of the night.

WINTER'S EVE

5

The sky is an abandoned circus tent,
confetti still falls through naked wires.

Smoke from machines of light
almost sings like a calliope, the one

I love still beats in my blood
like footsteps in the snow

anyone can read.

DUST DEVIL IN THE PARK

It pounces out of bright air, dark,
spherical, & livid with men & women

chasing blankets flapping off, a
quick red hallucination of flags,

a nameless hunger stalking,
its only tracing atoms pink & gold

coiling above the grass, ripping open
packets of loose dust & veering

into the north of two white girls
& their breasts, warm as grackles banking

down from cottonwoods to fields.
From a fold in the sky comes the blush

of mystery in our thoughts when spirals
connect us to our childhoods

& we speak of how much we needed help,
how much anger we still hold for help ungiven.

Any generosity to our children heals
like the yellow cry of swallows over ponds.

CORRESPONDENCE

Gaslight glows
purple like veins
throbbing in the undertongue
& blood burns.
Inside a gull's creaking pinion,
coalminers stare, cracked
from the windshield of a Ford.

We listen to birds & rocks,
the first songs are there.
In old times they walked
& knew a more webbed light
flowing through each stone.

They remembered the riverbend-
with-three-saquarro-cactus-place.
We say "road,"
entering that mist
as if for everything we say
something is erased in Heaven.

A black dot in the sky
becomes an immense shadow
cast by the archangel;
what was a pinhole of light
becomes the human.

I STILL HAVE MY FOUR THORNS

—for Rosy Sky

We began as lemonwood saplings,
stretched bows, two arrowing arms aimed east

into carnation dawn, after prom night
red & white crepe streamers twined from balcony

to stage, the motif, ships that pass, memories
we were using to improvise in dance class,

all night at the lake, the guys in rented tuxedos
falling drunk off the wharf, too scared to say

goodbye, & we breaking thorn branches to be
blood related, not surprised to find sunrise

in our wrists, & in those veins every hooked
fish & burnt child made us sweat, two waking dreams

in tights, two black roads diverging, connecting,
the whole double odyssey shined on by that

dark sun you kept seeing that spun off rose drops,
& returning through the circuit to tell me

there is nothing immortal, only this music
coming through the silence of you gone

swirling into Asia with someone, torn programs
announcing our world tour, the one slow turn

our bodies would scribe in unison, our edges gone
electric with the gold stars of kindergarten,

sunsets with the perfume of you, each pebble,
each hurt foot healed, nothing only itself.

KABUKI DANCE

These lacquer eyebrows,
cheeks scored with black lightning,
call back the power human faces once had.

Our story a storm like a winged lion
blows the village apart, our fathers
snapped out of the green

singing in the tall grass. The liquids
of their eyes boiled as they stared into the fire
where lizards writhed

through a crown of light, the passage back
sealed by the sun. We scroll the sky
with the speech of drums.

We freeze the most volcanic look. We show
the change as a slight shift
of our fans.

even in this dump.'' ''When are you going to get it
through your thick skull . . .'' Duhamel would say,

poking her forehead with his finger. Frances would
fly into the apartment, come out swinging a framing

hammer. ''Touch her again, I'll brain you,'' she swore.
Duhamel'd go inside, throw himself down on the iron

bed, reach under the mattress to the cardboard port-
folio where the coin of the moon dropped into

the jukebox of night & made cricket music come out.
''I wish I were stronger,'' Marie cried. ''There, there,''

Frances whispered, rocking her in her arms.

THE ONE WHITE HORSE

December wind makes a tin drummer sound.
Horses graze on chamois-colored grass
& in the mountains, antelope

of snow. Here come the canada geese again,
& the planet is taking us somewhere
because the one white horse

stands in the center. December wind makes
a tin drummer sound & calibrates magpies
to fenceposts to empty ears

of milkweed. What is the soul of a horse?
Does it die? Does it go on cropping winter
grass even after its rack of bones

falls unstacked? Three girls cross
the field like sunset-red cranes,
given these benign days.

A sudden health is staggering for a moment.
The planet is taking us somewhere
because the one white horse.

DRIFTWOOD, THE MUSE & LADY LUCK

It lies on sandy rocks,
the flotsam heart of something huge
& nearly extinct, a mammoth butterfly breathing
in the rise & fall of waves,
its grain pocked like a carnival barker's hat,
the spiel promising heaven in the beat
of forty-eight hooves pounding turf.

This stump is you, father,
the weathered roots your forepaws curled
around the wheel of your cummins diesel rig,
clamshell purple under your eyes
from driving all night to Jersey City
for the morning line, the Big Exacta, the dream
you never gave up
& even as the doctors pulled the tubes from your arms
you were only the more free to crowd the rail.

A spider's thread
dangles from your hull
like spittle from a played-out thoroughbred.
It hurts that you hoisted me up
to race across what you left unloved for Lady Luck,
fading like sunset behind a toteboard.
To love something distant & unappeaseable
is to cheat death, you said.

Here, on this inter-tidal zone
I weave seaweed garlands for the Muse
to lure her out of the sea for a song.
Far off the coast

another tree stands
ready to begin the long migration.
It smells of salt & mushrooms
rotting in a limestone cave where, drop by drop,
a great obstruction is dissolving.

SHROVE TUESDAY

The same old women
who lit candles thirty years ago
in my parish pray in red-stained light,
their knuckles like knots of tarred rope
in Lisbon.

My sons stand near the altar,
a glass coffin with St. Teresa's effigy inside
covered with dresden roses. They wheel,
open-mouthed, staring at the painted dome,
sick with Jesus whipped & crowned with thorns.

When the nuns catechized me
they asked, what are the evidences of God?
Here, I would answer
Spring's sudden bloom, the bellshaped thrushes
who arrive from an invisible shore,
singing up dawn, making ships appear in the bay,
flags astern, evidences of other harbors
through which we sail, through which we will return.

I remember singing
"blackbird, blackbird, in & out my window"
as we wove under Sister Mary Elizabeth's wide sleeves
knowing who the blackbird was, & later,
writing letters to the Blessed Virgin,
which we would burn,
sending our petitions up in smoke to her address.

This evening
my sons & I stroll San Pedro beach

sharing what we saw in the thieves' market —
prehistoric radio tubes, duelling pistols, field glasses,
cracked plaster Jesuses —
when we come upon a lungfish, gasping,
hauling itself across the sand
on pectoral fins.
I see my sons as babies
crawling across the kitchen floor.

The surf roars outside my window,
a white moon hangs in the sky, pulling at my blood
with an ache like a flying sheet of glass.
Tomorrow the ashes, the incense, the burning.

THE HALLUCINATION WAR

In the small cove at San Pedro
coalseams fork like black silver shrouds
through rock. I trace the orders of antediluvian fern
& the sound of the waves revives the old thirst
for a whiskey.

Down the strand, a stone column
breaks from the headland to stand alone
like an Easter Island face, staring forever skyward.
The cliff walls glint with bits of glass inset
in cement—seahorse, scallop, sailboat.

American music from the cafe
brings me up the steps. A line of warships
cruises out of Lisbon harbor. The radio says China,
invasion. Perhaps the final war
my sons are certain of has come & the earth
is going deliriously inside itself like a gypsy
seized with glossolalia.

In the wall, a little shrine
untenanted by any saint is hollowed out
with words inlaid of stone:
          ao deus desconhecido, it says,
               to the god unknown . . .
The sky is brittle like the inside of a kiln
lined with blue tile.

THE SLUMS & THE KINGDOM OF BABONIA
                —for Jack

The sun rose.
The children came out of their cardboard shacks to play.
One boy chased another, swinging a dead rat.
A girl grabbed it,
chased the stunned boy
until they spotted you, & crowded 'round,
cooing & touching your hair as if it were leaves
from a gold plant.
You stood it a minute, then bolted.

It's alright, I told you
as you trembled in my arms.
I used to be one of them, part of me always will be
somewhere in the summer of '48, playing guns,
crawling through blackberry bush jungles
& above, in elm tree coconut blinds
snipers waited for us to wander into their crosshairs
& ping! one of us would be down in the weeds,
creased in the forehead.
As we rumbled home from swimming at the reservoir,
mothers inched toward their children
as if we were Huns.

Remember the walk we took
up the hill to the coastal battery of guns
& we happened on that herd of goats?
We crept through the underbrush
to watch the young ones butting horns
& you whispered, "I used to be a goat on the planet
Babonia, but the old King told me I have to be
human here on Earth."

A dungeon look passed across your brow,
& you added, " . . . unless things get really bad."

Your mother says I should tell you both sides,
& she's right. The kids I grew up with
called me four-eyes, sometimes beat me up.
I told her only the bad things
to excuse the pain I sometimes am
& forfeited whatever didn't fit the story.

It's alright.
Those kids, they're thistles
which grow in any hemisphere in any weather,
prolific, thorny, touched with a purple
lovely as dusk.
Take some of that, mix it in.

from

Crying in the Cheap Seats

Duerme, no queda nada,
Una danza de muror agita las praderas
y America se amego de maquinas y llanto.
—Federico Garcia Lorca

IN THE ENDLESS POEM
I wonder sometimes what the connection is
between the poem and the world.

Do I expect the world
not to kill or maim me?
not explode my house of ecstacy?

Do I expect an end to the murder of children
their bodies thrown in ditches
ripped by phosphorous bullets?

This endless poem is a song: someone
somewhere hears its syllables.

The melody makes moments yet alive
and makes us frightened too of other harms
we do ourselves
                as when, if
we would wait alone for execution scared into silence
and never make this fragile and temporary music.

     In the endless poem
we are in death row: it is vast
and contains
the world.

MY TOWN IS CALLED SOUTHBRIDGE
its streets and gutters
run with the rain
of my memory

every space in it definite enough
to be a place
has an episode of the endless poem
hidden like a demigod in it.

I make my Via Dolorosa
through the cobbling streets of this town
how it flowed into me
how the outside world like the Quinebaug River
flooded my town of ecstacy
away.

BOYS AND GIRLS IN A CIRCLE
around the grave of a cat

an altar boy in his black cassock
saying Our Father quick in latin

they all go home to supper
he digs up the shoebox casket
of the cat he killed by throwing it
in the trash-barrel fire

puts the body on the tracks
where the 5:30 local
squishes it to fur   pulp   blood

what does he see
crouching over it
poking it with a stick?

They tell his mother
and she takes his hand and
burns it on the stove

how do you like it
she asks.

THE COURT WE LIVE ON IS A DEAD END:
a cyclone fence
and then the light and power company

a hundredfoot smokestack
coal burns   the sky is grey sometimes:
all night the transformers hum like locusts
to the sleepless

sitting on the steps I can see them all
the mothers   leaning out over railings
hanging clothes on spiderweb lines
from second-story porches in housecoats

battling against the soot
screaming across the street "Chris d'Calvie!"
when one kid gets beaten up by another

they wash and cook
and love their husbands one night
throw them out the next, sometimes saying
how they've been to confession to take
communion and no making love
hulking husbands stinking beer

and as if the Church were not enough
they go to a woman's house on Worcester Street
who drops two drops of olive oil on water
and if they join it is the reason   the evil eye

a lot of them work the second shift
at the American Optical
I see them cutting down the sad path
        through the coal yard
and theirs is the death of cancerous mothers
and retarded children to be sent away to Belchertown

but mostly   it is this picture
a mother shaking out a rug
on the back porch on a blue May morning
the month of Mary

she sings some simple song.

STRANDS OF PEOPLE'S LIVES BEGIN TO
braid in the poem.

The mean kid stoned the skinny kid
on the crown of his skull   the blood
was fire in the forest of his hair
it streamed as he ran to his mother
crying through the weeds and burr.

The mean kid years later
stood at night with me in the coalyards
asking me to please teach him
words   And it was a clear starry
night and I said the word for that
was "obituary."

The skinny kid is sitting on the veranda
of the country club   collapsed
draped in a blanket soaking wet crying
begging saying
"I couldn't save him, he was too big,
he would have . . . I tried!"
his dark hair wet with another blood
his big idiot friend I saw   his body
delicate as beached jellyfish
his face puffed up   his mother
old in her thirties the mother of thirteen
children and a drinking husband   stared at it
her arms crossed under her breasts   her breasts
only covered with a threadbare sweater
smelling the smell of fish as if
dying there had made him aquatic
weeds and the mud at the bottom of ponds
reeking from his grapplehook-punctured body
and said, ". . . good enough for him."

WHEN I WALKED IN GLOBE VILLAGE
the rhythm of the Ames Worsted Mills
the cloth being warped and woofed
with a clack and a clack
the bobbins spinning   their threads eaten
by the looms   frames   shuttles
a finished product spewing out on rolls
like an endless textile tongue

people were working   all the summer windows
were opened in the heat   the men the women
worked   I could smell their sweat
they leaned out of doorways for a draft of air
and waved hello wishing they were young like me
and wanting me to have my rightful childhood.

The Quinebaug was dammed above the Globe
and the woolen plants poured their dyes
red and blue and green
                              and swimming in the river
I would come home clownish in mottled flesh.

All these things passed into me
and I am their loom
endless, endless
they dyed they weaved the patterns
these workers   eating supper at 5:30 with their families
in their homes on Hamilton Street

I felt they were my mothers and fathers too
adults   mysterious   smoking cigarettes
they would feed me I knew if I asked
I see these people in wet bathingsuits
on Sunday afternoon picnics at Cedar Lake
fully grown   erect   sharing their laughter

My mind is sultry rainstorms on these
bricked castles on the river:
how can   how should I   deny them?

AFTER SCHOOL I SPEND MY TIME
down by the Quinebaug River

down past the coalyards
the river runs hard
in lists between huge concrete blocks

they were going to erect
a trestle for the Grand Trunk Railroad
on those blocks

"They died on the Titanic, those people
that owned that railroad," my mother said

I hear the steamwhistle over the North Atlantic
busted bulkheads   the iceberg horn
panic and song   the ark of lights goes dark under

and so they left these concrete things
unfinished, the paws of sphinxes.

These human associations
this residence in the earth
mix flesh with the wood and stone of
our habitations

the thin fingers of a sampan woman
I see her cooking beans on an open fire
moored along a Chinese river

she knows the endless motion has worn it
thin on the stone mortar
grinding grain

she knows the grinding motion
of sex   the endless summer
of the tropic

just as the hawk knows the poem of flight
his eyes blaze with a man pleasure
his wings outstretched over a global updraft
the lady wind swirling
to make a hollow into the nest of the earth

the Quinebaug the North Atlantic the Yangtze
endless flowing flowing through now

JACK KEROUAC'S FUNERAL

     Where's St. Jean Baptiste Church?
a sunoco gas station
at the end of the Rt 495 cut-off
DOWNTOWN LOWELL the sign

Oh, Saint John da Baptis'?
Hey Harry (over the door H.H. Johnson)
where's Saint John's
                 a guy draining the oil
of a car on the lift yells
jus' keep goin' til you can't go no more
turn lef' an' you're on mer-mak street
that's frenchtown, up abouta halfamile

the second part is
finding jean baptiste in a rundown
wounded neighborhood
gaping spaced lots waiting for urban renewal
like an old hag waiting for false teeth

stop in a coffeeshop
cupacoffee at the counter, readin' the Lowell *Sun*

        suffering a massive hemorrhage
        a former Lowell *Sun* sportswriter
                    French literary
        prizes *Maggie Cassidy,* which tells of
        his life and times, in fictional form, at
        Lowell High School
                  On the Road
        "beat" refers to beatific
                 a bridge
        between the Lost Generation . . . and the heirs of
        the Beat Generation, the hippies (sure)

                educated at Lowell . . . went on to
                Columbia in New York where he played football
                (me too, me too)

guy comes in
give me the two crull-er, eh? an' cof*fee* to go.
frenchtown.
                    I thinks of Maggie, the scene where
he's sittin' on the can and she's blowin' him
tryin' to get him to stay home instead of goin' off
to college, he wantin' the city, writin'
leavin' her and the life of a railroad brakeman behind

yeah, I thinks, this is where
the tenement three-deckers
the backlot pickup baseball games in the twilight
before the mothers callin' kids home
to fridaynight fish fries
and the omnipresent sacred heart of Jesus calendar
hung on the inside of the bathroom door
in french naming the saintsdays
are
        an' wow here's the merrimack river
rocks and the riverwater's in the three channels
Jesus! I thinks, just like
southbridge I knew it

across the street from the church
a young guy says, They're goin' to have it
at eleven   I says Where's the home
(meaning where'd the Kerouacs live) but
he says up the street at Archambeault's

so the third part is
in archambeault's funeral home
where I come back into the real french-canadian
idea of class
                        a room marked Mr Jack Kerouac
and there he is, in the casket

the place is empty except for this
like maybe crazy college kid standing against the wall
with a funny smile on his lips
I kneels and prays (one for Cynthia) looks and
jesus jack you are still there, your
soul? yes, soul, is still there

you look mighty like my uncle pete
in your bowtie and check jacket, rosary beads
clasped in your hands (badly crinkled)
and your classic features, greek statue lips
long straight nose
                        noble, remember?
WORK LOVE SUFFER Kerouac motto
next to the bier a coupla dozen roses shaped into a valentine
the red satin ribbon bearing the gold legend
GUARD THE HEART
                                    who sent it?

guy comes in   whips off his winter jacket
plunks down on the pew   wrings his hands
sighs loud tears O JACK I MADE IT JACK

mrs kerouac, stella, comes in
the guy comes up with rheumy words
are you mrs kerouac   I'm VERY sorry
holding her right hand in both of his
until she pulls it away

tight jaw and dry eyes
deep lines and black depression trenches
in her face, the veil, anguish
like shot in the stomach but tryin' not to cry out

Ginsburg comes in with Corso
(a long navyblue coat rasputin wore)
allen stands bending at the waist talking
to mrs kerouac saying how he and Gregory
will make a movie about the funeral
and she looks up   she says

Do what you want
but I never want to see you again

and he bows (quiet guru) and goes to Corso
and the sound of the goddamn camera whirring

out on the street I hears the merrimack
rushing over its rocks
standin' on the high bridge the wind
bright with October morning blue sky
                                        I hear
boys in bathingsuits yelling running barefooted
over 1935 rocks
a lowell tech kid walking by says
don't jump, christ, do I look that bad
                                        I see
jack straying along the river thinkin'
about serpentine monster in the core of the planet
getting ready to rise, its sulphurous snake-eyes springing
into the atmosphere of lowell and rising
like a rocket menacing the cellstructure of the universe

it rises and rises
until it falls into innocent atoms
                            poor Emerson
only Dr Sax *knows*

there's a three-decker
with clotheslines of sheets flapping white
and jack is up there
with a jug of wine, only
it's the GREAT AMERICAN NIGHT and stars
like headlights cruising down turnpikes of eternity

jack is gettin' a little high
lookin' from off that rooftop to the river
thinkin' of his old buddies
sampas, maybe, thinkin' of who and what
regrets, finally remorse
loving God in the mountains of Washington
burnt out on his friends in frisco
buddha burns in the shacks of berkeley

go on loving, dying somewhere between
the artist and the man   take your choice
be a artist or a human person
                              the artist
will make a movie of his friend's deathtime
I thinks, judge not lest ye be judged
ginsberg is just then driven into the parkinglot
behind the church
judge not   WORK LOVE SUFFER

the next part is the funeral
father morrisette speakin' with the fren'chaccent
of the sins of Israel (judge not)
so beautiful he prays
please Father forgive your servant Jack
for any sins he may have committed in this life

in black vestments with gold trim
the church high vaulted ceilings, paintings of the saints
and jean, john, jack baptizing in the jordan the young Christ
Are you the messiah?
No, I am but a voice crying in the wilderness.

The eulogy
                Jack lived around here and came to this church
                Even when he was a boy he used to come
                to the rectory and talk about how he wanted to write
                to express the feelings he had in words

                We encouraged him
                He left us and went out and made a great name
                and wrote his writings

                I read his books
                some say his books are indecent
                but I could see that they were a great force for good
                because Jack had a vision
                of the freedom of the human spirit
                and he spoke against every form of bullying he met

                now he is at rest

said father morrisette and I guess everybody just knows
jack's going to heaven to be with gerard

around the casket shaking the censor
incense rising to the rhythm of the bells
holy water beading up on the bronze
the old man with the crucifix   leading the procession to the doors

the casket down the steps
into the tv camera
denise in cloth coat, creeley
a reporter takes jimmy breslin's statement

and the last part is
out at the cemetery down along the avenues of the dead

mrs kerouac, no tears, not once
the priest, I am the life the resurrection
tv cameras churning   Corso's camera whirring
mrs kerouac leaving as soon as the final
syllable of the glory be evaporates

Ginsberg handing the camera to Creeley
he using the one eye into the eyepiece
a shot of Corso Ginsberg laying a yellow carnation on the casket
the eternal celluloid record
                                        I guess
Creeley is another true artist

drivin' down south home through towns
stow and bolton and marlboro I hears Jack sayin'
All American authors are insane   you gotta be crazy
to be a writer in this country

angelheaded hipsters in the starry dynamo
of the night all mad for life generating this
spontaneous bop prosody

exactly one year before
I write
                Dear Jack,
                        please don't die
                        write more books instead

now he is at rest
and I'm goin' home to make a poem
of Jack's deathtime
I'll just keep goin' til I can't go no more
turn lef' and there he'll be

I WALK OUT INTO THE WINTER NIGHT
to think about Kazantzakis' "Cretan glance"

and the endless poem brings me to
Breen's Bar in Worcester
with friends in a booth drinking
talking
                one friend says Dylan Thomas
is *the* great modern bard
the other says Thomas is "just
a manner of speech"
and he begins to roll out carolling syllables
loud as the bartalk   the barflies buzzing
to hear him matching the participial momentum
of Dylan's Welsh mind tumbling down into the harbor

"Jesus Christ!" the first one says,
"if I had one tenth the talent
you're just pissing away I'd be up in my room
writing like a bastard. What the hell are you doin'
drinking your life away?"

"Let me alone, then," the second one says,
"I am what I am. I can't and won't be anything
to please you or anyone else."

            The endless poem
is a long walk toward Cretan caves:
something about death
something about facing God and death
and all the unanswered questions
with courage and without insolence.

from
The Anarchist Heart

GHAZAL

Black under red sunset the mountains release
the ghosts of feelings I never let myself have.

Once, when I couldn't help my children accept death,
the mountains went invisible under a blizzard.

The rock of what I learn to live alone with,
whatever won't go away is the mountains.

Wave on wave of leaving, the mountains are
the wife leaving the husband, the husband leaving the wife.

The mountains make me kneel in my garden
& confess to seeds my only satisfaction is work.

At evening the mountains are potted geraniums
because in me a love of beauty still lives.

JANIS JOPLIN & THE INVENTION OF BARBED WIRE

All morning grey flints of wind shoot
down from the foothills across the horse pasture
behind my house. Tumbleweed hard as coral
bangs against the lapboard, scratching at window panes
with the quilled fingers of caged men.

I see them on porches after supper
listening to wind pour over the grasslands,
their minds spinning & creaking like windmills
drawing waters up from underground.

This range full of unsettling music
& they, bright wingtips of sinful kisses,
sagebrush burning on lips of prairie night,
waiting for thunderheads.

They will string wire on cottonwood stakes,
draw squares on the land's pure curve & at dusk
return, asking nothing of their wives
but to bank fires & lay down in cactus beds
while they go dying, meteors in the whiskey town.

A woman stomps rhythm there in gold shoes
shouting "get it while you can" through the fence
that owns her voice. She dies giving birth,
flowers of Texas darkness still pinned to her dress.

Clouds rush by
like herds of ghost buffalo.

SONG FOR JEANNIE

This is a song for you about you
& around you like a minuet cocoon of tenderness
& regret.

Jeannie, everything on this planet
is going to die, the computers are humming
the limit a hundred years.

I told my son Ben
that scientists say
our sun will super-nova,
swallowing us with its blessing
of hydrogen corollas & love
five billion years from now
& he cried like any limit makes tomorrow.

I think his tears now
& suddenly everything is important, even the wards
for the prematurely wise.

I remember the night when I met you
& you were dancing about the flower in your womb
& it was a delight that strengthened me against
the streets of New York with their bombs & dollars
& wine bottles of murder.

I remember the night we sat near the fire
the first summer of the lake
& you spoke of the rising & rising again of the flashlights
to meet the restless dead parts of ourselves.

I remember the rainbow headband you took off your waist
for me, the sweat & the grapes & the devoured
men in your tent.
I remember your hair demanding a hill facing sunset
with the will of your deceased bank-account
& I remember how you hugged me & said you loved me
when you knew I thought you insane

& that's the shiv in my spine,
that we all thought you there,
where you walked out the door,
out of the white corridors & the shock treatment

& I can see you walking back into that fireside
talk astonishing us with all your time travel & prophecies
in children's rhymes

& I have this vision of you running in a hospital
smock over the Hudson River
in a narcosis of headlights toward the century
we have left
                    where all the broken marriages
& destroyed Californias, the desperation to find
father, mother, child & the Holy Ghost in one man
who will not kill you with his dying,
his black whiskers of photographs
& his boyish smiles
                    all count, very much.

No dream of whips & multiplication tables
will black out the sun, which will be with us
till we end.

It doesn't matter whether we do it in forests
or on tugboats in the oily harbors,
that exquisite hunger in our centers
to live, to eat life,
that lovely & grieving appetite is it—

what we are, in brilliance, hymns of comets,
is it, what we *are* kills us.

It matters & it doesn't matter
if all is cloudless skies of penance.
Nothing is there between touching
& needing to be touched.

What you suffered before us, the cold
floors of your fight with the economy of love,
that there is never enough, like there is never enough Moses
or bread.
            Your nursery school rooms are
            festooned with alphabets & zebras.

So this is the endsong of the one who knows
living is dreaming the fire of your cells
quavering over the dead lakes.
Every nightmare & betrayal, every half-catholic
half-jewish prayer, every coveted fur coat
& cheap rhinestone matters now
as a stick in the house-of-beginning-to-be
is subracted by the wind.

The song & the fire will sleep like a fern
in the rock, the silence before the next movement
stirs on the bows of Heaven:

dance, little flower of the womb, dance now!

THIRD SON
    —for Jack

The night you were born it was morning
before we came back into time.
Your contractions arrived, irregular
& of themselves, surging & astonishing,
until, despite the doctor & his theoretical clock,
your mother knew.

The moon had gone down
& we crossed the river into the small city
with its sleeping hospital.
We could feel you inside, rising,
your mother & I together touching
the clenched sheath which held you.

In delivery she grasped
the steel railings, my hand,
anything to work against,
her vaginal lips fiery & opening for you.
She & I were breathing together
as if for the first time,
holding hands, talking.

When your mother strained hard in labor
her eyes seemed like two knotted boles of an oak
& her face changed.
"You look like my mother now," I said.
"If I look like your mother," she gasped,
"then you're seeing yourself be born."

It was like that, sudden words
spun me back to a dream I kept having

before you were born.
A woman would say to me,
"Somewhere in America we reach the border,
& we are driven outward & beyond ourselves.
Don't worry if you die. I will give you a new body."

Your mother took two deep breaths & shuddered,
your head appeared, lightly tinged
with clots of blood & hair.
The nurse put silver nitrate in your eyes
& you cried softly & turned to us
cupping your ear as though listening.

I drove home that morning
watching the rising sun flesh out the trees
& felt blessed, knowing nothing makes it any easier
to be human, believing I would no longer be divided
& struggling against myself.

The struggles have not ended.
I have taken the world into me
& the armies of darkness & light forever
march toward each other in my fears & hopes
whenever I write. But this morning, the morning
you were born, I had this vision
I could be messenger.

If you wonder why I look at you & smile
unaccountably sometimes it's because I see that.

TO WILLIAM BLAKE

A man is marking a grid in chalk
on a blackboard.
He then begins making asterisks
at co-ordinates until he has a constellation.
He then commences to weep.
Then scream.
Then pound his fist into the spaces between stars.

Another man walks into the room.
He looks at the blackboard, he looks at the fist,
he looks at the scream. He shakes his head
& walks away.

It's the same now. Two
dimensions, a flat plane, &, if I leap
into the blackboard with its geometry of God,
perhaps three.

When will I accept my angelic form?
I'm tired of the steely demon who waits
until my dog dies & I stand by the highway with her
in my arms, while my neighbors scrape her
a shallow grave & her bowels void
so that I cannot wash that stench away
& my memories of her loving, eager eyes are
mixed with that foul smell.

I too wish to awake from the sleep of centuries.
Lately, I've been seeing the tobacco auras
of my students & doing doubletakes so often
they think I'm crazy.

Cynthia thinks I'm a doppelganger.
She says this leads to prophecy
but can't say how.

We hold each other as close as a man & woman can
when the woman's eight months gone.
Outside, a fog covers the Atlantic seaboard.
I rub her aching back
& this is the same as the child
I will love & have loved since that night
last summer in the pine-grove.

Last night I was thinking of two friends,
a man & a woman; their forms began to swirl
behind my closed eyelids & there appeared
a giant eye, the iris of which spun,
heaving off webs of flame

& I thought of you,
merging with the object.
But for me this happens only through a go-between,
a pregnant woman's aching back.

Does this mean I'm a peon of the imagination?
Black bread, a wooden bowl, a cheap wine drunk?

I think America is sleeping like Albion.
A dark sleep, vast as the plains
where the eye should see
over the horizon.
I touch her shoulder in the night.
She makes some muffled protest.
She ain't in the mood.

Ages & ages pass.
Giants rise out of the desert.

Cymbals of brass. I become an ape,
chattering among rocks. I watch the flower children
wilt. Watch them hustle in Brighton,
trying to scrape enough together for their sopers.
None of them anymore enchanted
by a guitar.

The people are burning for wheat.
Is this your apocalypse? Yesterday I saw
the billions of the Earth make a human chain
around the globe. What do you make of that,
William?
We have sent a rocketship to Jupiter
Saturn & beyond, bearing the legend of humanity,
the male & female forms into deep space.
My mother told me we are Iroquois people & believe
the humans fell through a hole in the sky
to this ocean planet,
a turtle in great circles making the continents
for feet to stand upon.

I have seen the billions marching,
a great human parade into deep space
falling through holes in the skies of new worlds.
What do you make of that, William?

Tonight I believe
the whole of art to be
the contrivance of endings. In life
we know better. In sleep
we fall through a hole in another
world: the dead dogs rise
with radium eyes

to haunt the White House.
We reach for a stone fireplace when ten
constellations spin on summer nights.
The Aurora Borealis
is humanity
marching into deep space
& still there is that aching back
that must be soothed.

I'm sitting at a pine trestle table
seamed with the boiled flesh of bulls
& grieve for the trees & animals that fell into it,
& even what with the consolations of philosophy
I know I'm not supposed to (for chrissakes,
William, somebody's always trying to argue you out
of your feelings) & look, I want to be
as transcendental as the next guy,
but what do I do with my heart?

Someday I hope to be equal to making a poem
about the tragic waitress of the Maverick Diner,
her bruised eye against the glass
as she dishes endless pecan pie
to the raving drunks before dawn.
This poem is like her,
a night shift, a red star over the vitamins.
The poem will simply end when the booze runs out.

Blake, bloke, bleak, blanch, blatant bugle,
you time have come, man, rise!

One more pull & that's it. Fleas
biting my ankle. The dog is dead but the fleas
survive. What do you make of that, William?
Me? I'm going to stay in the game
until the hand's all played out, the royal flush,
one time, O God, please,
before the end.

YOUR FATHER'S DAUGHTER

In the old photograph he leans, foot poised
on the runningboard of his black Model T, a thin
young student at the college of agriculture,
his eyes still bright with the apple orchard dream.

His father dies.
With one shoe-factory job or another
he supports his wife, his mother, a little girl,
paying the mortgage on his father's dream,
penny by penny, double-shift by egg-money
through Depression.

When you were a girl during World War II
he planted apple trees behind the barn, nurtured them
for years until they bore.
Neighborhood kids broke into his small orchard that Fall,
climbed the trees, cracked off branches,
shook down the apples, threw them at each other,
all laughing, falling in the grass.

He came home from work,
saw his hope of having one place for himself
in ruins, went into his shed, got an ax,
chopped down the apple trees, swearing & crying
as they crashed to the ground.

I think of you the summer
you planted pansies near our campsite
& late one night drunken poets trampled
your one bright patch of purple & gold.
You began throwing dishes, pots, smashing the flashlight

cursing & crying for a place of your own
where flowers can bloom
& no thieves break in.

It's sunday afternoon, December, 1944.
Deep snowdrifts surround the red barn like raw silk
& your father hammers a rocking-horse together for you
out of old orange crates, making up with skill
& labor (scraps of leather make the pony's
tail & mane) for what he lacks in cash.
You look back on his life
wondering what he might have been,
an artist perhaps, a magician with junk, an inventor.

That New Year's morning
later, when you worked in the city
watching your landlord stumble drunkenly
singing his way up the driveway into his new day
you knew you were not Lois Lane
& Superman was not coming to save you.
Your father's yankee lesson took.
You would not wait for life to make its gift
before you made your own.

You say you made a place for me
to be an artist & with whom were you keeping faith?
I say we carry our father's, our mother's lives
into the next stanza, hoping to learn
a simple kindness, the gift of time & space,
an orchard, a flower, a poem.

THE COMMUNITY

At the little carnival
for the old Laurel School,
my kids were doing the cake-walk
to mariachi music & tossing rings
& trying to knock the swinging pinata
into a blizzard of candy.

I was watching the 12-year-olds
the boys chasing the shrieking girls
like sexual fireflies across the schoolyard
breaking water balloons in their hair.

One slim girl came to rest near the doorway
soaked by that special boy
so that her tiny breasts stood out
molded against her red nylon jacket
& she leaped up, kicking out her legs
& cried, "Yiii!"

An old Mexican gentleman,
seeing me see her—he pointed to her
with a quick jerk of his chin
& winked at me.

DISNEYLAND

> "Eternity opens from the center of an atom."
> *—William Blake*

An abalone shell boat carried me
down the black corridor, almost forever.

With a sound of tropic evenings & sleep,
a man's voice spoke to me.

Snow fell in sheets of diamonds,
snowflakes with cities lit up inside them.

I entered & saw the molecules,
globes within iridescent globes,

feathery, globes like angels' faces in the ballroom of night,
whose one orbit is the limit of time.

I saw all the little bars of America, the world,
all of us whirling around the proton mother,

worlds, hot orbs of sexual music inside us,
gunning down highways, crashing into each other,

all of us like drunken guests circulating
around the absent host, never able to fall in or out.

The nucleus itself, the pulsing heart,
crystals of knowledge pumping through glass arteries.

The voice says "You may not enter."
I cry out in the love of the purified tornado of starless space,

the last circling of van Gogh's ravens,
Buddha's god saying "end your desire."

At the microscope's rim I see the eye
examining me for my birthmark.

Stammering I crash into potted palms in motel lobbies
trying to tell them what I have seen.

The guests steer clear of me.
No matter. The buses of Anaheim will take them.

I'll wait for someone going wretchedly to pieces
thinking they ought to be able to stop it.

Perhaps my words will be enough.
I'll speak with the sound of tropic evenings & sleep.

THE ANARCHIST HEART

You were the only Canuck left
the mills couldn't grind the Canada out of,
living up by the hemlock woods, the deer run from
Vermont to the Sound, running a 12 mile trapline.

You showed me the almost chewed through
ankles of mink willing to limp three-footed
out of the iron jaws with their lives.

Me & your brother,
winter nights we'd smoke cigarettes
in the dark house, turning the radio knob
searching for a new sound
we heard one night—
The Moonglows singing "Sincerely"
so much bluer than the McGuire Sisters
we jumped up and down, breaking the bedsprings
& laughing ourselves empty
until in the renewed quiet we came back to
the only things real—
the Korean War & Paulie's sister
whose body made our balls throb
& whose favor meant having every bone
cracked by Paulie who could lift
a Beezer over his head & who vowed
he'd never stand to hear his sister called
the town pump.

But you found her favor
& Paulie he picked you up & beat you
against the stucco walls of Bob's Sunoco
then sent your blacked-out body up
on the car lift
& when you woke you were in the air,

falling off to the grease stained floor,
opening up your skull again.

It was for that you joined the Marines
& when they wanted to make an airplane gunner out of you
you said, no, I got to feel the ground under my feet.
Hitch-hiking back from Parris Island
lighting out into the woods with a 30-30
& a book of matches.
Sonny, they would've never caught you
if they hadn't've staked out your mother's house,
figuring you to come see her one night.

When the cops took you away in the squad car
you winked at your brother & me.
They got you to Philly
before you cold-cocked the MPs
in the terminal men's room & made your way home.

I wanted to kill the government bastards
when they caught you again at midnight
with a string of rabbits slung over your shoulder
as a gift to your mother, to make some ragout.

They sent you to Walpole
& something got into me, I couldn't laugh about it
no more. You were mine & the forest's
& the cops were foreign soldiers
more strange than the Russian troops
we imagined parachuting at night
like poisonous mushrooms, taking the country
as it slept while we would strike out for the woods
to form a guerilla army & take back our land.

I saw the cops coming & coming
until they tied you up in iron & made you live
their way. They weren't alien invaders,
coming in spaceships. All the movies
about intelligent beings with no hearts were no fiction,
science or otherwise.

I used to think you were dumb,
that you went on laughing on visiting days
because you didn't know someday soon
you'd kill the last mink in Massachusetts.

I remember how after you got out,
we went to celebrate at a roadhouse in Fiskdale
& you stepped out drunk on the highway
when a Cadillac knocked you sixty feet in the air
& you just screamed in the gutter,
"Bring me my handgun!"

I've been thinking about you again,
how you took my breath away the first time I saw you,
rising, naked, out of the millpond
with a dozen bullfrogs tied around your waist.

It never mattered how much the cops
would come after you & after you,
you'd come back to it & back to it,
til the end, not hating them anymore than
hating yourself for setting your traps
or God or whatever arranges for Cadillacs.

I think of you limping through your woods
singing a quadrille. Me, I sing my song & gnaw my
ankle for a while, & sing my song.

from
Home Front

CADILLAC KEYS

Your wife called me into this; everything
was flying to pieces, she said. But I
knocked on your door with the limping

      fist of a man with no clear right
      to enter. All I could hear was a hail
      of claws attacking the hardwood.

         You were charging her father's Christmas
         table on your wheelchair, arm-swiping
         lamps to chalk, screaming for

      the keys to the Cadillac. She was
      punching you on the prison record.
      You smelled of rubbing alcohol, piss

& rage. A man in a wheelchair without a car
is no man at all, you thought—
not if after four days of nembutol sleep

         you had to have more & she
         had thrown the keys into Framingham.
         Your dreams are walking;

      waking is when the surgeons tell you
      another part has been taken away.
      You are wheeling inside me now, the thin

thin legs of you streak through me
like gulls at the beached narwhale of Revere.
Some crippled part of me is tearing

my heart, my lungs, the man inside
turned teeth. The social worker came
with the papers

      & you burned him: "You & your 10-cent psychology.
      What do you know about pain!" You buried
      his head between your knees

& made him confess he believed in nothing
but the electrocution in your thighs.
When the cops came to take you

you slipped to the floor like an anaconda
with a man inside it, fighting them til they
whipped you bloody with handcuffs. You weren't

      crazy you yelled, it was just the
      pain the old hands at the rehab unit
      said would get to you someday, when you became

      a centaur in Florida to show them
      the book of your syringe, damned
      if you would die howling in sanitariums

like your aunt, the leper of bad luck
& south Boston white ghettoes. I love
your childhood with its potatoes

      dug out of Maine rock that hardened
      your nails against the thievery of the Portland banks.
      The look you gave me in the squad car

      said my day would come. You made me
      ride through the whiskey & bad contracts
      that feather my spine. I am

afraid of you
like I am afraid to live. I can tell
your wife still has dreams of you stripped of all

      suicide, writhing on the jailcell floor
      hissing "revenge." I can tell
      she stared at your gifts, smashed

         the Christmas tree lights flashed on
         & off. I can tell she desired to
         reach through her uniform to what was you

that burning bone, what holds against these
accidents that bring us down, that
comparison in our lives I had escaped

      the flesh of, that falling into the sleep
      when we let the bad debts go, & let
      the keys, for the last time, go

         til we're used up, til the dead wall barring
         the country that's standing inside us
         crashes in the sleep that brings us to ourselves.

SONG OF THE BRUTE

I am
a brute. I was made
to haul grainsacks in boxcars
on shoulders too big to be born.

I can't figure out
how to get cars out of mud—
something about slabs & jacks.

When I see
light by the water place
in morning it is silver pitchforks
their tines pinning me open.

When a breeze
lifts the oak branches
down three hills
it is my wife
walking toward me.
She sees gold flash on my right.
I see them. We do
not talk at night, the stars
shine through the smoke-hole, the tent
poles. This is not like the field,
the sky is a cone, no trails to reach them.

Here they all cross at my wife's sex,
the stars sail. I know
it is the earth
moving.
I clutch dirt
hands under the fireplace stones
in terror of the brute.

COMING ACROSS

Nebraska summer cornfields endless
& boring like a pregnancy long overdue.

Strong coffee, pancakes,
after a night in Lincoln, the generous land
frondescent under the bell of the moon.

Under our tires interstates turn to black bread,
our trailer banging in back
like newlyweds' tin cans.

And pressing on up
through hills past Ogalalla, Julesburg,
nearly asleep at the wheel picturing new people

leaning on a jukebox in some cafe
we ran off the road, dust dancing around us
with feathered fans.

In the sere grass the cattle listened
to the immense dry stillness of this inland sea,
the radiator fizzing.

We squatted by the roadside
running dirt through our fingers,
feeling waves lap our wrists with a slower pulse.

Just over the next hill, or the next . . .

HOME FRONT

—for Cynthia

Handing out anti-war leaflets at United Aircraft
I shouted, "Learn what the jets you build
are used for!" A Black held up his paycheck.

At home I wanted you to sympathize.
All those hours trying to teach a wider world.

You were busy with Ben.
Two years sick, he was a thin ghost.
Your spoon plane was trying to come in
for the thousandth unhappy landing into his mouth
with all he could digest—the same rice cereal
as yesterday & the day before, *ad nauseum.*

Tonight, remembering those days,
I also remember my father say to my mother
in the three-decker kitchen of my childhood,
"He better do good in school, Irene.
Him born blind like that, even with the operation,
he's damaged goods, he'll never do a man's work."

I'd hear Ben coming & wonder 'is he damaged goods, too?'
& couldn't bear to look at him.

This has nothing to do with the others
& why they tried to stop the war.
This has to do with when I stopped trying
to stop the war & went home.

EVENING WITH NOVELISTS AT CROWN POINT ESTATES

We are seated before the fieldstone fireplace in the carpets soft
as lambs' wool. Our host plays a tape. In it a Forward Air Con-
troller with an Oklahoma drawl directs a bombing strike some-
where in Cambodia as the bomber pilots break in with complaints
of taking heavy fire from a pagoda they are not authorized to
respond to while Nixon's speech declaring an end to hostilities in
Southeast Asia is being piped into their cockpits from Radio Aus-
tralia. The pilots are hip to the ironic situation. But they speak
excited as boys putting a stubblefield to the torch with the per-
mission of their fathers.

One of the guests stands up, calling the host a psychotic, a sadist
who enjoys reliving the kills, he can't stay another minute under
the same roof with such a monster, such a moral cretin.

The host protests. True, he's a veteran, but the tape is evidence
he would have used if Nixon hadn't been driven from the White
House by Watergate. Besides, he says, everything he could ever
say about a theory of fiction is embodied on that tape. Facts no
longer exist. The record is simply a fabric of conflicting fictions
which are believed in absolutely because not to believe them
would mean that everything we've done we've done wrongly.
That is our morality, the necessity to stick to our fictions because
the consequences would be more than we could bear without them.

It's obscene to maintain that you would have released this tape,
the guest replies. You wouldn't have had the guts! I suppose
you have to believe that, the host answers, smiling. The angry
guest storms out the door.

We understand them both.

The guest has been living in Europe for seven years. He hasn't
been in this atmosphere. He still believes that, like Neruda, he
can show his hands to the generals & say, "I am not part of this
crime." Everything for him is simple as an inquisition.

We can relate to our host's passion for complicated narrative tech-
niques, his vision of blizzards obliterating all the trails of blood.
We see through the fiction of innocent, non-complicit lives; per-
haps to have been born is itself the fundamental crime. A taste
for the theology of the counter-Reformation is rekindling here;
Goya's prints are enjoying a widespread revival.

The party goes on.

CARRYING AN OAR INLAND

Lying in bed this morning
we recall the last things we saw before sleep—
two bank towers flashing time & temperature
& office lights left on,
outlining their I-beam skeletons in dark.

Those people in Pittsburgh
welding beams from rolled stock in protective masks,
their children to be sent through school,
friends, unforgotten lovers, fistfights in boot camp,
all going into these buildings,
the deep structure of the town made visible
like remembered dreams.

Like last night
I dreamed that Taoctl,
brain surgeon to the royal house,
passing the ante-chamber of the Temple of the Sun,
overheard the King tell the white man
of the White God's prophesied return.

The white man shouted a word
which hissed like an iguana, Blasphemy!
He broke the image of the sun, the mask with green eyes
without which men go blind.

Taoctl knew then his world was ending.

Nowhere to go
but back into the rain forest
to open himself to the jaguar's scalpel
or listen to the wind in the northern desert
to learn what other beings may teach men
whose calendar has been smashed.

The doorbell rings.
It's a woman from the Jehovah's Witnesses
with her little girl listlessly leaning on her mother's hip.
She tells us to get ready.

FALL

Long marsh reeds
nod on the riverbank, surrounded
by willow leaves turned brown.

They've let go.
Like a businessman giving over
the company he began.

All night the leaves have been
riding the Poudre by. Summer they burned
to add one cylinder of cells
to strengthen the stalk
for coming snows.

It has happened—behind them
their hands were molting at the wrists—
in the turbulence of a passing cattle truck.

They forecast the Arkansas as they pass
& finally the bright blue gulf where they might go,
parts of some chalk world they always knew
was forming there inside, filled with
mountains & currents & flying, undersea.

VICTIMLESS CRIMES

As a child I believed God
the same as fists my blackened eyes
could not deny. Objective he was
in the sandbanks across the tracks & beyond
the Quinebaug River from St. Mary's.

The second article of my faith
was God in baseball games, movie marquees,
long division problems, mandolins
& my neighbors singing
"I'm Looking Over A Four-Leafed Clover"
in broken English on July nights.

I'd sneak out the bedroom window
in my underwear to catch the moon
on the light & power company transformers
& hear them turning into mushrooms
releasing their electron spores down the lines
in clouds.

Therefore, it was up to me
to get my heart right to see that shine
snowing down the nave of thunderclouds like manna,
the sheen of elm leaves at noon,
the town clock banging the long midnight out
over the jailhouse where anybody could be
as Jesus said in the Beatitudes.
To stalk the moment
when sunset on the Spectown Diner windows
was God smiling would require humility.

I first looked at my own body
when it was my turn to be the werewolf

& saw hair bristling & heard the lunatic howl
broadcasting for someone to see me
red & magnetic with the charge.

Twenty years
before I saw William Blake
hitch-hiking in his buckle shoes
carrying a hand-lettered sign saying
"What the eye beholds, that it creates" on one side
& on the other, "They became what they beheld."
I cracked up on the off-ramp to Hammond, Indiana.

Through the smoke I could hear a dynamo
chanting beneath Lake Michigan
& tonight
in the vibrato of the refrigerator
it sings, "You're already dead. God squashed you
like a cockroach years ago.
I doesn't make the story up
& I doesn't get the story down.
There is only the watching & soon
the bones settle out from each quarter of the heart
& make a dense fossil you can read
like a french novel razored open
in which you get arrested
for the victimless crime of spiritual voyeurism."

I'm released this morning.
At the edge of a stubble-field a man is crying
"Hide! hide!" to a flock of wild geese.

We walk home together through the dry March snow
which has knotted up in scales, spotted black & white
like the back of a whale shark
that has just given birth
to the world.